A billiard table decorated by G. E. Magnus and supplied to Queen Victoria. It can now be seen at Osborne House in the Isle of Wight. (Photograph by David Cockroft, reproduced by gracious permission of Her Majesty the Queen.)

BILLIARDS AND SNOOKER BYGONES

Norman Clare

Shire Publications Ltd

CONTENTS

Billiards and snooker 3
In the beginning 5
Early billiard tables 9
The development of the modern
 billiard table 11
The billiard cue 17
The balls 23
Marking boards and scoring boards .. 25
Billiard table lighting 28
Unusual billiard tables 30
The origin of snooker 31
Places to visit 32

Published in 1996 by Shire Publications Ltd, Cromwell House, Church Street, Princes Risborough, Buckinghamshire HP27 9AA, UK.
Copyright © 1985 by the estate of the late Norman Clare. First published 1985; reprinted with amendments 1996. Shire Album 136. ISBN 0 85263 730 6.

Printed in Great Britain by CIT Printing Services, Press Buildings, Merlins Bridge, Haverfordwest, Pembrokeshire SA61 1XF.

British Library Cataloguing in Publication Data: Clare, Norman. Billiards and Snooker Bygones. – (Shire albums; 136) 1. Billiards 2. Snooker I. Title 794.7'2'028 GV899 ISBN 0-85263-730-6

This billiard table, made by G. E. Magnus entirely of black ebon slate, is on show at Penrhyn Castle near Bangor, Gwynedd.

A billiard table illustrated in the 'School of Recreation', published in 1710. This table is probably more typical of the billiard tables in general use at the period than Louis XIVs table (page 6), which would surely have been of superior quality. Both tables are of light construction, as the table beds were made of wood, slate not being introduced until much later.

BILLIARDS AND SNOOKER

When billiards was originally played the table did not have any pockets and only two balls, one for each player, were used. The game consisted of 'hazards'. A 'losing hazard', scoring one point, occurred when the player's cue ball struck his opponent's ball and then went through the hoop or pass, whilst a 'winning hazard', also scoring one point, occurred when the player caused his ball to strike and then drive the opponent's ball through the hoop or pass. The game seems to have concluded when the winner reached the agreed total score of three, five or seven points up (later of twenty-one up) and then by causing the player's cue call to rebound from the opponent's ball and strike the 'king post' or 'peg'.

The third ball, coloured red, was intro-

duced in France during the eighteenth century, when the pass and post were discarded. The continental game then consisted entirely of making 'cannons', a cannon being achieved when the player's cue ball strikes each of the other two balls in succession, so scoring one point: this is the game of billiards as still played in France, the rest of mainland Europe and those parts of the world where continental colonists have settled. There is evidence that when the pass and post were first abandoned the French also had billiard tables with pockets but they were evidently soon discarded.

The English game developed when the red ball was introduced from France in the late eighteenth century, pockets (called hazards) having been introduced earlier. The pass and post were now discarded. In Britain, with three balls on the table, cannons scored two points and in addition both winning hazards (now called 'pots') and losing hazards (now called 'in offs') were played into the pockets instead of through the pass. 'Potting' or going 'in off' the opponent's white ball scored two points, whilst the same strokes involving the red ball scored three points. These various strokes can be combined making a total of sixteen different combinations of scoring strokes. Five of these are the basic strokes: a *Cannon*, when the striker's cue ball hits each of the other two balls in succession — two points; *pot white* (white winning hazard), when the striker's ball drives the opponent's white ball into a pocket — two points; *in off white* (white losing hazard), when the striker's ball hits the opponent's white ball and then goes into a pocket — two points; *pot red* (red winning hazard), when the striker's ball drives the red ball into a pocket — three points; *in off red* (red losing hazard), when the striker's ball hits the red ball and then goes into a pocket — three points.

These five basic strokes can be combined in various arrangements, as follows: a cannon and pot white — four points; pot white and in off white — four points; a cannon and pot red — five points; pot red and in off red — six points; a cannon (hitting the opponent's white ball first) and in off white — four points; a cannon (hitting the red ball first) and in off red — five points; a cannon, pot white and pot red — seven points; a cannon (hitting the opponent's white ball first), in off white and pot red — seven points; a cannon (hitting the red ball

first), in off red and pot white — seven points; a cannon (hitting the opponent's white ball first), in off white and pot white and pot red — nine points; a cannon (hitting the red ball first), in off red, pot red and pot white — ten points. In addition penalties are awarded for various foul strokes.

There are twenty-two balls on the table at the start of a game of snooker: one white cue ball, fifteen red balls (value one point each), and one each of the pool colours — yellow (worth two points), green (three points), brown (four points), blue (five points), pink (six points), and black (seven points).

The game consists entirely of winning hazards, that is potting the balls. The player is obliged to pot a red before selecting any coloured ball to pot; the reds remain off the table after potting, but the coloured or pool balls are replaced on their spots until all fifteen reds have been pocketed, following which the colours must then be potted in order of points value, commencing with the yellow. The colours when pocketed now also remain off the table. It is always essential to hit the ball which is to be potted directly with the cue ball, otherwise it is a foul stroke. Penalties are awarded for various fouls; the minimum penalty is four points, but it is more if a ball of greater value is involved.

A 'snooker' is a situation when the striker cannot play a direct stroke on to the ball which he must hit. Thus one player will try to leave such a situation, where the opponent may fail to hit the ball, therefore committing a foul and giving points to the opponent who had caused the snooker.

The game of paille-maille, from Strutt's 'Sports and Pastimes' (1801). Strutt asserts that billiards is the same game as paille-maille but played on a table instead of the ground. Streets called 'Pall Mall' in English towns probably indicate where this game was played.

4

A French woodcut depicting shepherds playing a game on the ground in 1480. This seems to be evidence that billiards was originally played on the ground, as the woodcut clearly shows the boundary surrounding the playing area, the 'hoop' or 'pass', the 'king post' or 'peg' and the implements used to propel the balls.

IN THE BEGINNING

A great many games depend upon the use of a ball or balls and many such games that are now quite different from one another probably had a common origin. It seems likely that most games were originally played out of doors, although possibly some were played on a board or table and then adapted and enlarged for playing in the open air on a court or field.

The origin of the game of billiards is obscure. It has been attributed to several different countries, including France, Spain, Italy and Britain, but despite much research its source remains unknown. Charles Cotton in *The Complete Gamester* of 1674 wrote:

'Billiards from Spain at first deriv'd its name
Both an ingenious and cleanly game
One Gamester leads (the Table green as grass)
And each like Warriors try to gain the Pass

But in the contest e're the Pass be won
Hazards are many into which they run.'

However, in the same book he attributes the game to Italy, saying: 'The Gentile, cleanly and most ingenious game at Billiards had its first original from Italy and for the excellency of the Recreation is much approved of and plaid by most Nations in Europe and especially in England.'

Encyclopaedia Britannica records that a game similar to billiards was seen by a traveller called Anacharsis in ancient Greece about 400 BC and also suggests that Catkire More, a king of Ireland during the second century AD, left behind him fifty-five balls of brass with pools and cues of the same material, but this seems very unlikely.

Some writers give the credit for inventing the game to a French artist, Henrique Devine, who lived in the reign of Charles

An engraving by Antoine Trouvain showing Louis XIV of France playing billiards. Comparison with the 1480 woodcut will reveal that this is the same game as that shown in the earlier illustration — brought indoors and raised to table height. The implements used to strike the balls are 'maces', resembling those used by the shepherds.

IX (1560-74); possibly he had a part in formulating the early rules of play but there is no evidence that he invented the game.

Bouillet, in the *Dictionaire Universel des Sciences*, ascribes the invention to the English, saying that the game appears to be derived from the game of bowls. There are, however, reasons for thinking that the game is of French origin: even the French word *bille* (meaning billiard ball) seems to provide the first syllable of the word 'billiards'.

Strutt's *Sports and Pastimes* (published in 1801) states that billiards is the game of paille-maille played on a table instead of the ground. Others suggest that the game of croquet is a form of outdoor billiards and that both billiards and croquet have evolved from paille-maille. Certainly you can see the 'hoop', 'pass' or 'port' and also the 'king' or 'peg' in early illustrations of billiard tables and these items still exist in croquet but have long since been discarded from the billiard table.

Although the two games in their modern forms may seem very different, there are a number of similarities between billiards and croquet. Both are stationary ball games and the striker has sole occupancy of the field of play, the non-striker being a passive spectator who cannot influence the result. In both croquet and billiards points are made by 'breaks', thus requiring accurate positional play to make the next stroke easy. A knowledge of the angles of rebound is required and playing the striker's ball against a non-striker's ball and then going through a hoop in croquet is surely the same as going 'in off' in billiards.

That billiards was originally played on the ground is indicated by a French woodcut of 1480 depicting shepherds playing a game on the ground and clearly showing a boundary around the field of play, a hoop or pass and also a king post or peg, as well as implements used to propel the balls. An engraving of King Louis XIV of France playing billiards in

6

1694 is clearly depicting the same game, but now being played on a table.

It is known that billiards was played in England during the reign of Elizabeth I as Shakespeare in the play *Anthony and Cleopatra* (Act 2 Scene 5) has Cleopatra saying 'Let us to billiards, come Charmian'. It is also recorded that, whilst a prisoner shortly before her execution in 1587, Mary, Queen of Scots, complained to her confessor, the Archbishop of Glasgow, that her *table de billard* had been taken away by her captors.

RIGHT: *The Duchess of Burgundy playing billiards in 1694. The hoop or pass is clearly visible, but if there is a king post it is hidden behind the gentleman player. The table is of light construction and has pockets; this is the earliest illustration of a billiard table with pockets and a pass.*

BELOW: *This late seventeenth-century French billiard table is possibly the oldest still in existence. It belongs to the Rothschild family and has been restored as nearly as possible to its original appearance. It has a wooden bed and six pockets which are just holes in the table, the cushion rails are mitred at the corners. When pocketed, a ball tips forward the hinged brass hand beneath the pocket, where it is held until retrieved, when a counterweight closes the hand back against the opening through which the ball was delivered.*

7

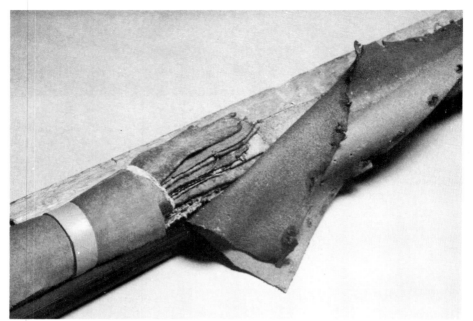

ABOVE: *Part of an old cushion rail, clearly showing the layers of felt or list padding, which improved the rebound of the balls.*
BELOW: *Two gentlemen playing billiards in 1704. There is a pass and six pockets but the king post has now been discarded.*

8

This billiard table of 1770 is much larger than the earlier examples illustrated and has eight legs. The hoop or pass remains in use and the table is still quite primitive, having a wooden bed and stuffed cushions. However, although the striker is using a mace, his opponent is holding a cue.

EARLY BILLIARD TABLES

When the game of billiards was first brought indoors it was probably to enable play to continue during inclement weather and it may have been played on the floor until somebody had the idea of raising the game to table height for the convenience of the players.

Early billiard tables were of very light construction as the table beds were then made of wood and they did not therefore have to support a very great weight. The plain wooden edging around the table bed was to prevent the balls falling on to the floor, and somebody must have had the idea of fixing some padding around the inside of the rim to reduce the noise of impact between the wooden balls and the wooden rim — and also to improve the rebound, and this must have developed into the original form of cushioning, either made up of layers of cloth (felt or list), or stuffed with cotton or horsehair. The first tables with pockets as well as a pass were being used in the late seventeenth century, and the king post disappeared about this time.

At this time too the players used maces to strike and propel the balls. These implements are almost identical to those being used by the shepherds playing on the ground in the 1480 woodcut. During the second half of the eighteenth century cues gradually came into use, and opposing players in a game might well have used different implements. The hoop or pass was still in use.

About this period the two different disciplines of billiards developed. Hitherto billiards had been played with two balls only, one for each player, although three balls can be seen in the 1480 illustration of billiards on the ground. The game in France and other continental countries discarded both the pass and pockets and instead introduced the red ball, and so their game consisted entirely of making cannons, that is the player causing his cue ball to strike each of the other two object balls. This is the game still played throughout most of Europe today and was taken by the French and Spanish to the parts of the world which they colonised.

The British game also discarded the pass but retained the pockets. The red ball was introduced from France around

9

ABOVE: *A wooden-bed billiard table made in 1816 by Gillow, the cabinet maker of Lancaster and London. This design was Gillow's number 971.*

BELOW: *The complete wooden bed, in three sections, of a Gillow billiard table, in the private museum of E. A. Clare and Son Ltd, Liverpool. It is made of oak and the surface consists of panels about 8 inches (200 mm) square set into a wooden framing in such a manner that neighbouring panels have the grain running at right angles to each other in order to minimise the effects of warping and shrinking.*

10

the end of the eighteenth century and so instead of winning or losing hazards being played through the pass these shots were henceforth played into the pockets. Cannons were also played and this is the game of billiards taken by the British to those countries which once formed part of the British Empire.

There are still a few very old billiard tables with wooden beds to be seen in country houses that are open to the public. Most of these tables were made by the famous cabinet maker Gillow, of Lancaster and London, during the early nineteenth century. One of the best examples of a Gillow table can be seen on request in Dunham Massey Hall near Altrincham, and a complete wooden bed in three sections can be seen in the private museum at E. A. Clare and Son Limited of Liverpool. The wooden beds were usually made of oak but the one at Dunham Massey is mahogany.

When wooden table beds were first brought into use it would have been extremely difficult to control the balls, there being little surface resistance to slow the balls down, in contrast to playing on grass, and it was probably for this reason that the table bed was covered with cloth, green being the colour used as it was taking the place of grass. However, it must have been a fairly coarse material. Charles Cotton in his *Complete Gamester* of 1674 writes: 'The form of a billiard table is oblong, that is something longer than it is broad, it is rail'd round, which rail or ledge ought to be a little swel'd or stuft with fine flox or cotton, the superficies of the table must be covered with green cloth, the finer and more freed from knots the better it is — the board must be levelled exactly as may be so that a ball may run true on any part of the table without leaning to any side thereof, but what by reason of ill seasoned boards which are subject to warp, or the floor on which it stands being uneven...there are very few tables which are found to be true.' In these early days the rough cloth required ironing to keep it as smooth as possible.

THE DEVELOPMENT OF THE MODERN BILLIARD TABLE

The tables made by Gillow during the early nineteenth century with stuffed cushions and wooden beds were slow running and not very accurate, although by this date ivory balls had taken the place of wooden ones. Ivory, however, is subject to shrinking in dry conditions and swells in a damp atmosphere and so the balls were never perfectly spherical. The players were playing against the table and equipment as well as their opponent, large breaks were almost impossible and games of billiards were usually twenty-one up.

During the early nineteenth century billiards became very popular amongst the aristocracy and the Royal Family, but there were no specialist billiard table makers. A billiard table had to be specially made to order by a cabinet maker such as Gillow. John Thurston, a cabinet maker who had been apprenticed to Gillow, had set up his own cabinet making business in 1799, making domestic furniture and billiard tables. In 1814 he decided to specialise in making billiard tables and billiard room furniture. He was the first specialist and he introduced most of the important improvements in billiard table construction which are still used today.

His early tables had wooden beds and stuffed cushions, but he began to experiment with modifications, assisted by the opinions of Edwin (Jonathan) Kentfield, who is looked upon as the first professional player and billiards champion, being undefeated for twenty-five years.

The first major improvement Thurston introduced was the slate bed. It is recorded in his sales ledgers that a slate bed was supplied and fitted to a billiard table in 1826 at White's Club in St James's, London. Thurston now described his tables as having 'Imperial Petrosian Beds' but stuffed cushions still continued in use for many years.

At first the slate beds were only about

11

ABOVE: *An early example of a slate-bed billiard table by John Thurston. More substantial underframing was required to support the heavier weight of the slate bed.*
BELOW: *A billiard table made by Orme and Sons of Manchester about 1880. By this time the slate beds had reached a thickness in some cases of 2 inches (51 mm), so requiring even heavier underframing, which provided scope for wood carvers to display their skills.*

John Thurston
(1777-1850),
'father of the bil-
liards trade'. After
serving his appren-
ticeship to Gillow,
he set up on his
own in 1799 as a
cabinet maker in
Newcastle Street,
off The Strand,
London, where he
would make bil-
liard tables to
order. In 1814 he
moved his business
to Catherine Street,
also off The
Strand, and spe-
cialised in making
billiard tables and
billiard-room furn-
iture only. He in-
troduced many im-
portant improve-
ments in the con-
struction of billiard
tables, including
the slate bed and
rubber cushions.

1 inch (25 mm) thick, the same as the wooden beds they were replacing, but being heavier they were usually made in four sections instead of three and the construction of the table underframing became more substantial in order to carry the extra weight. The superior quality of Thurston's tables is attested by the fact that in 1833 he was granted the Royal Warrant of King William IV. Slate, however, is not absolutely rigid but is surprisingly flexible, and so the thin slates tended to sag if not properly and evenly supported on the underframing. As with wooden beds there was a tenden-cy for the balls to 'rumble' when rolling on the table surface. Both drawbacks were overcome by increasing the thick-ness of the slate beds first to 1⅛ inches (29 mm) and then to 1¼ inches (32 mm). They gradually became even thicker, finally reaching 2 inches (51 mm) thick, and so the supporting underframing also became more and more substantial in order to carry the increased weight. At the same time the wooden underframing was often beautifully carved, many fine examples being installed in gentlemen's houses during the late Victorian period. As a result of the increased weight the beds were now made in five sections.

The next important improvement in-troduced by Thurston, in 1835, was the fitting of rubber cushioning instead of stuffed felt or list. Strips of rubber were built up in layers to form the cushion, just as the felt had been. Many professional players did not like the new rubber cushioning because rubber in its natural state loses its resilience during cold weather. To overcome this problem hot water pans were provided, one to be placed against each cushion, to warm them before a game. The invention of the vulcanising process of combining sulphur with rubber brought the tremendous advantage that the vulcanised rubber retained most of its resilience in cold weather. Thurston was quick to realise how important this was and took out a

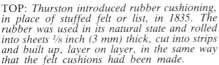

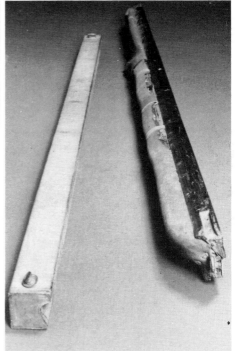

TOP: *Thurston introduced rubber cushioning, in place of stuffed felt or list, in 1835. The rubber was used in its natural state and rolled into sheets ⅛ inch (3 mm) thick, cut into strips and built up, layer on layer, in the same way that the felt cushions had been made.*

ABOVE: *In the early days the cloth covering the billiard table required ironing to keep it as smooth as possible. This billiard iron has a 'slug' which would have been heated in a fire and then placed inside the base of the iron.*

RIGHT: *At low temperatures natural rubber loses all resilience and becomes very hard. In unheated rooms during the British winter a table with rubber cushions would become almost unplayable, and so six hot-water pans were provided with the table. These would be filled with boiling water during the afternoon, so that billiards could be played in the evening. A pan is illustrated (left), together with a complete, stuffed cushion rail.*

16,328. Buttery, W. Dec. 13.

Billiards, tables for. Consists of an arrangement for preventing the cushion frame and rubber block of a billiard table from becoming loose, and for giving a more rigid groundwork for the rubber. The bed of the table is shown at D, and to this is secured the metal plate C by the screws E and nuts E¹, while to the plate is fastened the rubber blocks B by the screws G. The cushion frame A has slots H cut therein into which fit the projecting heads F of the screws E, by which arrangement the frame is easily placed in position or removed for tightening the screws.

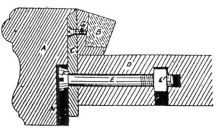

To obtain the best rebound of the balls off the rubber cushioning the rubbers must be mounted on a very firm and solid foundation. The 'steel block cushion', invented by W. Buttery and patented on 13th December, 1886, was a great improvement and was adopted and marketed by Burroughs and Watts Ltd of London. Many quite old tables are fitted with this type of cushion, which is still being manufactured today.

patent in 1845 for his 'frost proof' cushions. Once again he led the way and effected a very important improvement in the construction of billiard tables. He continued to supply billiard tables to the Royal Household, retaining the Royal Warrant of Queen Victoria, which had been originally granted to him in 1837. John Thurston died in 1850, the year before his work was recognised by the award of the Prize Medal in the Great Exhibition.

However, his successors continued his work and were granted the Royal Warrant of Edward, Prince of Wales, and later, when he became king, the Royal Warrant of King Edward VII. Shortly after the Billiards Association was founded in 1885 to establish and control the rules of play, the billiard traders were

A billiard table of plain design, such as would be used in clubs, hotels and billiard halls during the period 1900-50.

invited to compete by submitting examples of their work for inspection by the Billiards Assocation. In 1892 a Thurston table was selected as the standard which has been specified in the rules ever since.

Around the beginning of the twentieth century the game became popular in ordinary clubs, hotels and billiard halls. In such places tables of plainer design were required and so, apart from those of elaborate design installed in large private houses, most tables manufactured now had plain turned legs or plain square legs, these being not only cheaper to produce but also easier to keep clean.

There was a boom in the opening of public billiard halls during the ten years following the First World War, with a great demand for tables of plain design. This was followed by a depression and lack of demand during the thirty years from 1930 to 1960, although during this period the game of snooker became more popular than billiards.

Billiard tables of traditional design standing on eight plain, square or turned legs are still being made, with only a few universally 45 millimetres (1¾ inches) in thickness; this has been found to give excellent playing conditions and there is no advantage from using thicker slates, which have the disadvantages of excessive weight and greater transport costs. During and since the mid 1960s tables of more modern design, with built-in levelling adjusters and standing on plinths or pedestals, have been introduced. These tables are specially designed for ease of erection and future servicing and also to withstand climatic conditions in overseas countries where the services of skilled billiard fitters are seldom available.

A billiard table of modern design, with built-in level adjusters and standing on pedestals. Note also the modern lighting shade.

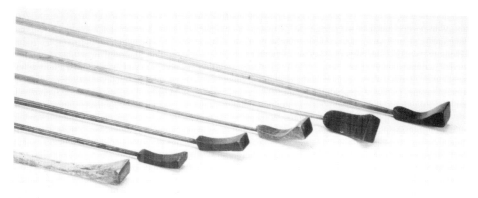

A selection of mace heads.

THE BILLIARD CUE

The implement originally used to strike and propel the billiard balls was called a mace. It remained the only instrument until about the middle of the eighteenth century although there were some variations in design. Some were made of a single piece of timber, usually ash, whilst others had a hardwood head fitted to a separate shaft or handle of ash or hickory. Sometimes the head was capped with ivory. The ball was struck a blow with the head of the mace and there was also a stroke known as 'trailing' whereby the player continued to push the ball until satisfied it was going in the desired direction before withdrawing the mace. The face or striking surface of the mace head was flat and the ball could only be struck at its centre point, thus the application of side, top or bottom spin was impossible. Later the shaft became longer and was then held over the shoulder instead of directly in front of the player, the mace head being slightly angled on the shaft in order to compensate for the fact that, being over one shoulder, the shaft itself did not assist in lining up the stroke; instead, a black sighting line was marked on the upper surface of the mace head to assist the player to aim correctly. Because the head was slightly angled to the shaft, it was necessary to have both right-handed and left-handed maces, examples of which can be seen in the cue racks at Dunham Massey.

During the second half of the eighteenth century, there being no rule to prevent it, a player might sometimes use the end of the mace shaft with which to strike the ball, especially when the ball was so close to the cushion that there was not enough room to use the mace head. Players gradually realised that many strokes were made easier by using this method and it became the accepted mode of play in Europe. So it was that, especially in France, the cue was developed and the mace began to lose favour, although either implement was used according to the player's preference. In the rules of billiards published by Hoyle in 1779 Rule XLVI states: 'When the parties agree to play mace against cue the mace player hath no right to use a cue, nor has the cue player any right to use a mace during the game or match without permission from his adversary.' Rule XLVII goes on to say; 'When a person agrees to play with the cue, he must play every ball within his reach with the point thereof, and if he agrees to play with the butt of the cue, he has no right to play with the point thereof, without permission from his adversary.' There

17

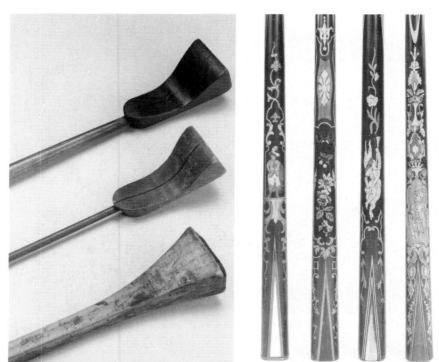

ABOVE, LEFT: *A one-piece mace and two maces with separate heads showing sighting lines.*
ABOVE, RIGHT: *By the end of the eighteenth century cues had become popular and their butts were elaborately decorated with inlaid designs and pictures. These cues in the museum of E. A. Clare and Son Ltd are of French origin, dating from about 1800.*
BELOW: *Maces with ivory caps to the heads.*

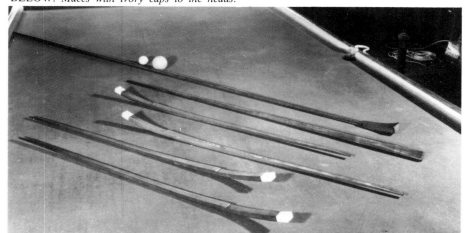

18

A billiard room scene depicted in marquetry work on a box lid. The right-hand player is using the 'wrong end' of his mace to strike the ball. This practice became widespread in the second half of the eighteenth century and the cue began gradually to displace the mace.

was indeed a period after the billiard cue had been generally accepted when either end of the cue could be used.

E. White, in his book *A Practical Treatise on the Game of Billiards*, published in 1807, says: 'The instruments used for striking the balls are two, the cue and the mace...of these instruments the cue is by far the most universal in use.' He goes on to say: 'The cue is the only instrument in use abroad...but in England until of late years the mace has been used almost universally, which the foreigners hold in the utmost contempt.'

An innovation attributed to a former French infantry officer called Mingaud, in 1807, was the fitting of a leather tip to the point of the cue. This simple idea, long since universally adopted, was probably the first important improvement in the equipment, as to a large extent it overcame the problem of miscuing when the point of the cue slipped on the surface of the ball.

The long prevalent practice of players using either end of the cue is the reason

for the chamfer which still exists today on the butts of most English-made cues. Captain Crawley, the author of *The Billiard Book* published in 1866, writes: 'The long tapering stick with which the ball is struck is called a cue. The best cues are made of thoroughly seasoned ash. The butt or handle should be well flattened on one side in order that it may be used to strike with when necessary.' However, in 1885 the Billiards Association was formed and established rules of play, one of which stipulated that 'the ball must be struck with the tip of the cue', but the governing body did not then lay down any specification of what was or was not a billiard cue and so many inventors tried to introduce improvements.

When necessary, maces with longer handles or shafts were used. Later, while it was permitted to use either end of the cue, it was not necessary to have 'rests' to reach the cue ball, but when this was no longer permitted it became necessary to use a rest and many ingenious rest heads

Fig. 15 shows the best position for playing with the butt; the left hand placed on the thigh, as here indicated, will be found of great assistance in steadying the body before delivery of the stroke.

ABOVE, LEFT: *Monsieur Mingaud, a former French infantry officer, is credited with the idea of fitting a leather tip, cut from old harness, to the point of his cue while he was in prison. This innovation was universally adopted, as it overcame the problem of miscuing when the point of the cue slipped on the surface of the ball.*

ABOVE, RIGHT: *Playing with the butt of the cue, an illustration from 'Practical Billiards' (1873) by William Dufton, a professional player. Either end of the cue could be used until the Billiards Association, formed in 1885, established the rules of play, one of which stipulated that the ball must be struck with the tip of the cue.*

BELOW: *A spring-loaded billiard cue, patented by A. J. Aspinall on 25th March 1886. The power of the stroke depended on how far the spring was compressed, and after lining up the shot the player 'fired' the tip end of the cue at the ball by pressing the release button on the cue shaft.*

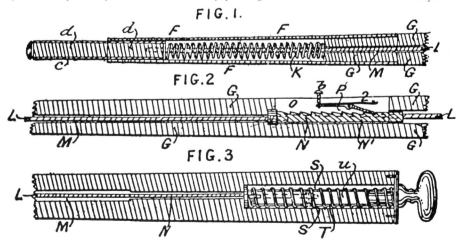

FIG. I.

FIG.2

FIG.3

(From left) Adjustable rest head; rest for one-armed player; swivel-type adjustable rest head; rest for one-armed player.

were designed. The present-day spider rests and span rests were introduced for reaching awkward shots.

It was not until 1938, following an incident at Thurston's match hall in Leicester Square, London, when Alec Brown was playing Tom Newman in the *Daily Mail* Gold Cup snooker tourna- ment, that a loose specification of a cue was introduced. Brown had found himself in a difficult situation and played a shot using a 'cue' about 5 inches (127 mm) long, which had been retained in his waistcoat pocket by means of a fountain pen clip. It had a tip on one end, which he duly chalked before playing the stroke.

Bartley's billiard room in Bath, about 1825. Bartley discovered that by striking the cue ball off centre he could screw 'in off' the red ball placed on the centre spot into one of the centre pockets, and his room keeper, John Carr, perfected the stroke.

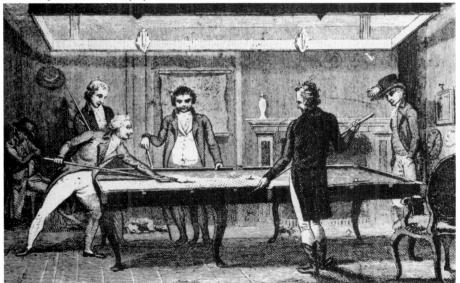

The referee, Charles Chambers, decided it was a foul: great consternation ensued and the rule book was consulted but he stood by his decision. Eight days later the Billiards Association and Control Club met and introduced a rule stipulating that: 'The cue shall be not less than 3 feet (914 mm) in length and shall show no substantial departure from the generally accepted shape and form.'

Although the cue was in general use and the cue tip had been invented during the early nineteenth century, players had not yet realised that by striking the ball off centre spin or twist could be applied. However, around 1825 a man called Bartley was the proprietor of a billiard room in Bath. He showed his room keeper, John Carr, how by striking the cue ball off centre, with the red ball placed on the centre spot and playing from left or right of the D, he could screw 'in off' into a centre pocket. John Carr perfected the stroke and then amazed the patrons, who always failed to accomplish this feat. He would then show them the secret, adding that it was also necessary to use his special 'twisting chalk' which when applied to the tip prevented mis-cuing when striking off centre, and he promptly sold small pillboxes of pow-dered white chalk at 2s 6d per box — equivalent to about £6 at today's value. Chalking the cue tip soon became stan-dard practice. By 1830 the application of 'twist' or 'side' was widely practised by good players and Monsieur Mingaud, the inventor of the leather tip, wrote a book published in 1830 entitled *The Noble Game of Billiards,* the title page of which states 'Wherein are exhibited Extraordin-ary and Surprising Strokes which have excited the admiration of most of the Sovereigns of Europe'.

LEFT: *Ivory balls had to be weighed and measured before important matches. These balance scales and the vernier gauge and ring gauge were used for this purpose.*

RIGHT: *A stack of twenty thousand billiard balls, the stock held by Burroughes and Watts Ltd in 1911, and then valued at £16,000. Two thousand elephants must have been slaughtered to provide the ivory for the balls in this stack.*

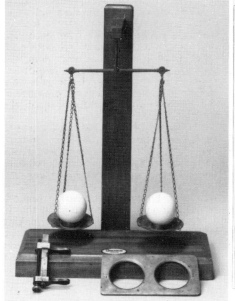

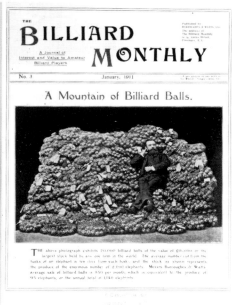

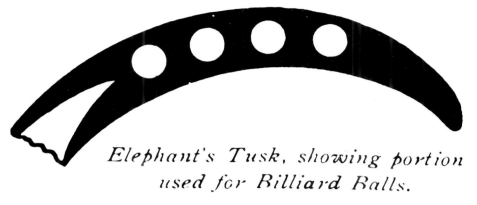

Elephant's Tusk, showing portion used for Billiard Balls.

The best ivory billiard balls were made from the small tusks of a female elephant, four or five from each tusk.

THE BALLS

The earliest billiard balls were made of wood. Even when new and made of hard wood, such balls would not be very true as a result of the shrinking and swelling of the wood according to the weather, and after a short time in play they would become very worn and rough.

It is not known when ivory balls were first used, although we know that ivory balls and also the ivory king post or peg were in use in the seventeenth century from references in *The Complete Gamester* of 1674. They must have been a great improvement with their hard shiny surface and pleasant clicking sound on impact with each other, and unlike the wooden balls they would not develop bruises or flat spots on their surfaces. Ivory balls, however, were hardly ever true spheres. There is a nerve running through the elephant's tusk, like the nerve in the teeth of all mammals including man. It was essential that the nerve should go through the centre of the ball from one side to the other, or else it would not be concentric. The nerve goes through the end grain of the tusk, and, like timber, ivory absorbs moisture and swells in a damp atmosphere and conversely gives up moisture and shrinks in dry conditions. The swelling and the shrinking, as with timber, takes place only across the side grain and not the end

grain, and so ivory balls were hardly ever spherical and needed constant adjusting while coloured balls required constant restaining for life pool and later for snooker. In addition, to obtain three balls of equal density and elasticity they had to be taken side by side from the same tusk. The best were made from the small tusks of female elephants and as only four or five balls could be made from each tusk only three were a good match with each other and the additional balls went into second grade sets. When important matches were to be played the balls were weighed and measured in the presence of the players and in full view of the spectators.

Thousands of elephants were killed to supply the demand for ivory billiard balls. The sales of Burroughs and Watts alone required the slaughter of well over one thousand elephants each year and there were at least forty billiards firms trading in London in the early twentieth century. Records of imports show that in 1890 some 750 tons of ivory for making balls was imported through London alone and more would also probably have arrived from Africa in other ports such as Liverpool. It has been estimated that to supply Britain with ivory balls required the slaughter of twelve thousand elephants in one year. Snooker, with its twenty-two balls in each set, was not yet popular but billiards was played throughout Europe as well as in most other countries of the world.

Fortunately, in 1868 John Wesley Hyatt of Albany, New York State, developed a substitute for ivory. It was the very first man-made plastic to be commercially marketed, made largely of cellulose nitrate and camphor loaded with finely ground animal bones and compressed and cured into a solid mass and finished by turning and grinding. An Englishman, Alexander Parkes, had made the same invention a little earlier but had failed to exploit it, but Hyatt formed the Albany Ball Company, registered his patent in 1869 and proceeded to market the 'Bonzoline' balls. They were far superior to and much cheaper than ivory but the players strongly resisted the adoption of the new ball. In 1900 George Birt, one of three brothers employed by the Albany Company, came to England and working with Percy Warnford-Davis commenced making similar balls there. These they marketed as the 'Crystalate' balls, but it took a long time for these composition balls to be accepted by the top amateur and professional players. It was not until 1926 that Crystalate balls were used for the amateur championships and 1929 for the professional championships.

The next improvement in billiard balls occurred during the late 1930s. Darryl Warnford-Davis (Percy's son) received word from the Albany Ball Company of New York that a brilliant German chemist, Dr Koebner, was in England and wanted to stay to escape from the Hitler regime. After some difficulty permission for him to stay was obtained and he introduced the process for making the modern cast synthetic resin balls, which are now produced in England, Belgium, the United States and Taiwan and have found universal acceptance.

A life pool marking board for nine players, with provision for holding the stake money in the glass-fronted vertical column on the left of the board, each player inserting his stake against the colour of his cue ball. On the left are two hand-held marking boards for spectators to keep the score on at billiards matches.

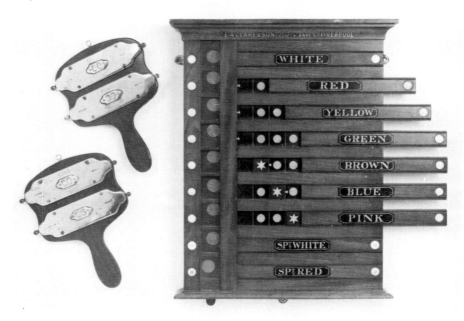

24

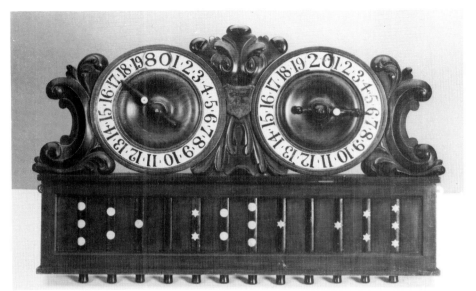

A marking board made by Thurston about 1815, and now in the museum of E. A. Clare and Son Ltd. Below the dials, which are for showing the score at billiards, is the early arrangement for marking the game of life pool, the source of the coloured balls used in snooker.

MARKING BOARDS AND SCORING BOARDS

The earliest marking boards were of the clock-face type, sometimes scoring only up to twenty-one, as in the early days with poor equipment it could be quite difficult reaching even this score. Charles Cotton in *The Complete Gamester* of 1674 states: 'the game is five or seven up when playing by daylight and three up by candlelight or more according to odds, but in gentlemen's houses there was no such restriction.' Many billiards scoring boards were combined with marking boards for the game of life pool, and these sometimes included provision for holding the stake money.

Life pool was unusual in that no points were scored. Each player had his own coloured ball, drawn from a pool basket at the start of the game. Having decided

what the stake would be, each player commenced with three 'lives'. When a player's ball was pocketed he lost one life, which was recorded by moving the slide to show one gold circular disc. When a player's cue ball was pocketed the second time the slide was moved to show the second disc: likewise, if his ball was pocketed a third time the slide was moved to show the third disc, and having lost his three lives he was now out of the game unless he elected to 'star' by paying another stake. This was recorded by moving out a slide showing a star one position. It was possible to star for a second time and in some circumstances for a third occasion and then the player was finally out of the game. The player surviving the longest was the winner of all

25

A large combined billiards and life pool scoreboard of the Victorian period. It shows the method used to mark the game of life pool for up to twelve players by means of slides, each marked with the colour of a player's cue ball. Many of these boards are still to be found in private houses and clubs.

Pool baskets. At the start of a game of life pool one coloured ball for each player was placed into one of these baskets, each player in turn shook the basket and tipped out one ball, which then became his cue ball for the game.

A clock-face marking board with a game counting device to enable the billiard room proprietor to know how many games had been played.

26

RIGHT: *Coin-oper-ated marking boards. On the upper board the score could not be recorded until a coin had been put in the slot; another coin was required when the score reached 100 points. The lower board has a variable tariff arrangement, re-quiring sufficient coins to tip a locking ba-lance in order to re-lease the mechanism. By placing extra washers on the other side, additional coins would be needed to tip the balance.*

the accumulated stake money.

Collecting the table revenue was al-ways a problem for the billiard room proprietor, who had to keep a check on the players and also on the room marker. Many of the early marking boards were fitted with counting devices so that the proprietor would know how many games had been played as a check upon the takings received. Some of these boards were designed so that they would not record the score until a coin was inserted into a slot.

LEFT: *A combined circular revolving cue stand with ball cupboards and folding marking board, which when closed displays life pool markers.*

27

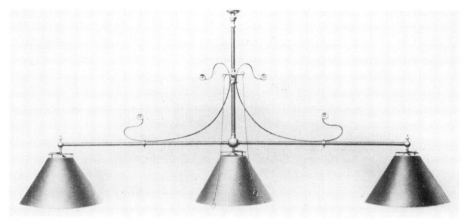

Three-light pendant gas lighting for billiards with anti-vibration incandescent burners.

BILLIARD TABLE LIGHTING

The earliest form of artificial lighting for billiards was candlelight. Charles Cotton's book *The Complete Gamester* (1674) contains the first reference to playing billiards by candlelight, stating that games were five or seven up by daylight and three up by candlelight, indicating the difficulty of playing with poor lighting.

Magnificent candelabra can be seen

Oil lamp for lighting a billiard table, fitted with a special billiard shade; from the catalogue of E. J. Riley, about 1900.

hanging over the centre of the table in the picture of King Louis XIV playing in 1694 and candles can be seen in other early illustrations of billiards. It is recorded in the magazine *The World of Billiards* that much light was lost by reason of the drip plates intended to keep the wax from falling on the tables from the candles at Thurston's billiard room in Catherine Street, London. During the 1830s the candles were replaced by Thurston with oil lamps and it then became necessary to suspend small saucer-shaped receptacles under the lamps in order to catch and prevent drips of oil from falling on the table surface.

Oil lamps soon displaced candles everywhere and references are made in old records to the lamps being set before important matches, and in one case there is a report that a young billiard room marker, when instructed to set the lights, had walked on the playing surface while wearing very heavy boots. Later the oil lamps were fitted with special billiard shades.

The professional billiards player John Roberts senior, in his book entitled *Roberts on Billiards,* published in 1868, recommends gas lighting. This was the 'ring and argand' type in the form of a treble T (a total of six burners) with the

28

'bat wing' type of flame, as incandescent mantles were not known until 1890.

Gas chandeliers, some very elaborately decorated, became the standard form of billiard table lighting at the end of the nineteenth century and into the early twentieth century. Charles Roberts, the champion of this period, son of John Roberts senior and brother of John Roberts junior, both of whom were also champions, in his book *Billiards for Everybody*, published in 1906, recommends the 'anti-vibration incandescent lighting' as being more economic than electric light and the best he has seen. The makers of this gas lighting also offered electric lighting pendants but the early electric lamps had a short and inefficient life. It was not until the first reasonably efficient tungsten filament lamp was introduced by William Coolidge in 1910 and his associate Dr Langmuir developed a gas-filled lamp in the GEC laboratories in 1913 that electric lighting became a practicable possibility for domestic and billiard table lighting, following which this form of lighting was universally adopted, usually in conjunction with circular, square or oblong reflecting shades. This was a very great improvement but there was still problems as the edges of the shades threw shadows onto the playing surface.

The next improvement in billiard lighting was in the shades. Various forms of inverted 'trough type' non-shadow shades were introduced during the 1920s and 1930s and are now almost universally adopted.

In the 1960s fluorescent lighting was tried but suffered two disadvantages. Colour rendering, important for snooker, was not very good and the stroboscopic effect on the moving ball was disconcerting, and so tungsten filament lamps were still preferred up to the late 1980s. At that time E. A. Clare & Son introduced low energy compact fluorescents, using 'cool white' tubes which overcome both the problems of colour rendition and of the stroboscopic effect. The other great advantage is that the running costs are lower, as the tubes are only 26 watts.

A billiard table decorated by G. E. Magnus, made for the Duke of Wellington. It can be seen at Stratfield Saye, the Duke's house near Reading. (Photograph by David Cockcroft, reproduced by kind permission of His Grace the Duke of Wellington.)

29

LEFT: *Thurston's octagonal billiard table of 1910, measuring 10 feet (3.05 m) long by 6 feet (1.83 m) wide. Two sides were much longer than the others and all six pockets were shaped like side pockets and set into the straight sections of the cushion rails. The design proved unsuccessful.*
RIGHT: *Between 1903 and 1912 Orme and Sons of Manchester marketed an oval table 10 feet 8¾ inches (3.27 m) long by 7 feet 3¾ inches (2.23 m) wide. It was of sound construction but a commercial failure.*

UNUSUAL BILLIARD TABLES

Monsier M. Mingaud, inventor of the leather cue tip, makes a brief reference to a triangular table in his writings of the early nineteenth century but this seems to be a most unlikely shape and we have no other reference to such a table. Most billiard tables were of oblong shape but a few octagonal, circular and oval tables were made. These were not successful, however, owing to the difficulty of judging the rebound of the balls.

A maker of some very unusual billiard tables was George Eugene Magnus, who was born in 1801 at Orsett, Essex, but moved in his teens to the Potteries district of Staffordshire, where whilst working for Josiah Wedgwood II he evidently learnt

the art of decorating and firing pottery. In 1838 he purchased an interest in a slate quarry in North Wales and another on the island of Valentia off the west coast of Ireland. In 1840 he patented a process of applying colour and glaze to slate and then used his skill to decorate household furniture and billiard tables made almost entirely of slate. He is known to have worked with John Thurston (their factories were close to each other in Pimlico and Chelsea) in making some very unusual and highly decorated billiard tables. One was supplied to Queen Victoria and can be seen at Osborne House in the Isle of Wight; another was made for the Duke of Wellington in 1842 and can be seen at Stratfield Saye, Hampshire. A Magnus table made entirely of black ebon slate (undecorated) is on view to the public at Penrhyn Castle, Bangor, North Wales, and one other decorated Magnus slate table is in private ownership.

The 'Multum in Parvo' (much in little) billiard table, introduced by Thurston's in the 1930s. 6 feet 1½ inches (1.87 m) long and 4 feet 6 inches (1.37 m) wide, it had two corner pockets, two 'middle' pockets (in one of the long sides) and three baulk lines. It was claimed that players could practise all the principal strokes they could use on a full-size table. However, it was not successful.

The cast iron under-framing and legs of a full-size billiard table made by Marsden and Saffley of Liverpool (note the liver bird cast into the end rail) between 1877 and 1880. These tables had concrete beds, one of which can be seen in the museum of E. A. Clare and Son, Ltd.

THE ORIGIN OF SNOOKER

The origin of snooker, unlike that of billiards, is well documented. Its history is recorded in articles written in 1939 by Compton Mackenzie and in 1941 by Colonel Sir Neville Chamberlain, who, as a young officer, served on the staff of Field Marshal Earl Roberts in India between 1881 and 1890, during which time the game was spreading throughout the British military stations. At this period, in addition to billiards, two other very popular games were played on the billiard table, namely pyramids and life pool. Snooker is based on a combination of these two games.

The game of pyramids requires fifteen red balls and the white cue ball. The red balls were set up in the form of a triangle (as for snooker) but with the apex red ball on the pyramid spot. One point was scored for each red ball until all fifteen reds had been pocketed.

The game of life pool is briefly described in the chapter on marking and scoring boards. It could be played by up to twelve players, who formed the pool, each having his own coloured cue ball delivered by chance from a pool basket. When twelve players formed the pool the coloured balls were white, red, yellow, green, brown, blue, pink, spot white, spot red, spot yellow, spot green and spot brown. When less than twelve players formed the pool then the number of balls was reduced accordingly. There was usually no black ball although there was another game called black pool which seems to have been the game of pyramids with a black ball added.

According to Compton Mackenzie, Neville Chamberlain, then a young subaltern, made the suggestion, whilst playing during the monsoon season of 1875 at the military station of Jubblepore, that to vary the game of black pool another coloured ball from the life pool set should be placed on the table, to which other pool balls with different values allotted to them were gradually added. At first, as can be confirmed by some of the early descriptions of the game, the positions and values of the balls varied and there would have been differences of opinion about the rules as they slowly developed, until finally a committee meeting of interested officers took place at Ootacmund in 1882, following which generally accepted rules became established.

Compton Mackenzie also records that one day a subaltern of the field battery at Jubblepore was being entertained by the Devon Regiment and in the course of conversation he told Neville Chamberlain about the soubriquet 'snooker' used when referring to first-year cadets at Woolwich. Chamberlain observed that the term was new to him but he soon had the opportunity of using it when one of the party failed to hole a coloured ball which was near a corner pocket. He said 'Why, you're a regular snooker', and then soothed the player's feelings by saying they were all 'snookers' at the game. So it was considered appropriate to call the game 'snooker' and it has been so called ever since.

Sir Neville Chamberlain writes that from the time snooker originated he travelled all over India on the staff of Field Marshal Earl Roberts and that they were constantly asked how the game was played. As everybody knew how to play pyramids, they simply showed how the coloured balls taken from life pool sets were added and told them of the simple rules which had been prepared at Ootacmund in 1882. So the game spread from one military station to another throughout India, assisted by the constant movement of military personnel, who carried the game with them to all the towns and cities and even to the remote frontier posts.

The game arrived in Britain when officers and sometimes complete regiments came home on leave and it is accepted that the game was first played in England at Woolwich Arsenal. Indeed, for some time it was thought that the game was invented at the Woolwich military establishment. The game spread into the London gentlemen's clubs as army officers home on leave or retired from military service either visited or became members of the clubs, all of which already had sets of pyramid balls and life pool balls. So the game was easily introduced and then slowly spread throughout the rest of Britain. It seems certain also that John Roberts junior, the famous professional billiard player, saw snooker being played during his visit to Calcutta in 1885 and would have brought some details of the game home with him.

Snooker however, unlike billiards, pyramids and life pool, was not recognised as an official game by the Billiards Association, which had been formed in 1885 to govern all the games played on English billiard tables. As the game gradually spread the Billiards Association realised that snooker had become permanently established and so during 1900 many committee meetings of the Association considered and amended the rules. Finally the Billiards Association formally agreed and decided to publish the rules at their meeting held on Tuesday 11th December 1900, but it was not until 1927 that the first professional snooker championship was held.

The game still took second place to billiards until the mid 1930s, when a billiard hall with fifteen billiard tables would require fifteen sets of billiard balls but only four or five sets of snooker balls. By 1940, however, this was completely reversed with five or six sets of billiard balls required compared to fifteen sets of snooker balls.

After the Second World War the popularity of black and white television caused the closure of many billiard halls. However, once colour television became available it was realised how suitable snooker was for this medium because colour is such an important feature of the game. As a result snooker is now by far the most popular indoor participant and spectator game.

PLACES TO VISIT

E. A. Clare & Son Ltd, 46/48 St Anne Street, Liverpool L3 3DW. Telephone: 0151-207 1336. Private museum.

Croxteth Country Park, Croxteth Hall Lane, Liverpool L12 0HB. Telephone: 0151-228 5311.

Dunham Massey, Altrincham, Cheshire WA14 4SJ. (National Trust.) Telephone: 0161-941 2815.

Osborne House, East Cowes, Isle of Wight PO32 6MY. Telephone: 01983 282511.

Penrhyn Castle, Bangor, Gwynedd LL57 4HN. (National Trust.) Telephone: 01248 353084.

Stratfield Saye House, Reading, Berkshire RG7 2BZ. Telephone: 01256 882882.

Billiard rooms and tables can also be seen at many other houses open to the public, including The Argory, County Armagh; Basildon Park, Berkshire; Castle Drogo, Devon; Cragside House, Northumberland; Dunster Castle, Somerset; Knole, Kent; Lanhydrock, Cornwall; Manderston, Berwickshire; Nostell Priory, West Yorkshire; Polesden Lacey, Surrey; Speke Hall, Merseyside; Standen, West Sussex; and Wightwick Manor, West Midlands.